BRETT
FAVRE

By The Staff of Beckett Publications

Brett Favre Uncovered
By the People Who Know Him Best

Copyright©1997 by Dr. James Beckett

Published by: Beckett Publications
15850 Dallas Parkway
Dallas, TX 75248
Manufactured in the United States of America

ISBN: 1-887432-35-3
Cover photo Courtesy of Pinnacle Brands Inc.
Second Edition

CEO/Publisher Dr. James Beckett
President Jeff Amano
Vice President, Operations/Finance Claire B. Backus
Vice President & General Counsel Joe Galindo
Director, Distribution Beth Harwell
Director, Marketing Margaret Steele

Editorial
Group Publisher Rudy J. Klancnik
Managing Editor Tim Polzer
Associate Editor Steve Wilson
Assistant Editors Aaron Derr, Joel Brown
Staff Becky Hart, Doug Williams (Photos); Randy Cummings, Tracy Hackler, Douglas Kale, Justin Kanoya, Mike McAllister, Al Muir, Mike Pagel, Mike Payne, Mark Zeske

Art
Art Director Jeff Stanton
Associate Art Director Eric Evans
Production Artist Emily Camp
Staff Therese Bellar, Amy Brougher, Bob Johnson, Sara Leeman, Sara Maneval, Missy Patton, Lisa Runyon, Len Shelton, Judi Smalling, Roz Theesfeld

Sports Data Publishing
Pepper Hastings (Group Publisher), Dan Hitt (Manager), Mark Anderson, Pat Blandford, Theo Chen, Ben Ecklar, Jeany Finch, Michael Jaspersen, Steven Judd, Eddie Kelly, Rich Klein, Lon Levitan, Beverly Mills, Gabriel Rangel, Grant Sandground, Rob Springs, Bill Sutherland

Manufacturing Reed Poole (Director) Lisa O'Neill (Production Manager), Ben Leme
Prepress Gary Doughty (Senior Manager), Pete Adauto, Andrea Bergeron, Belinda Cross, Marlon DePaula, Ryan Duckworth, Maria L. Gonzalez-Davis, Paul Kerutis, Lori Lindsey, Daniel Moscoso, Clark Palomino, Susan Sainz

Advertising Sales Jeff Anthony (Director), Matt McGuire, Mike Obert, Dave Sliepka; Shawn Murphy (Media Research); Lauren Drewes (Intern)
Advertising Inquiries (972) 448-4600 **Fax** (972) 233-6488
Dealer Advertising Craig Ferris (Manager), Louise Bird, Bridget Norris, Don Pendergraft, Phaedra Strecher, Ed Wornson, David Yandry (972) 448-9168
Dealer Account & General Information (972) 991-6657

Subscriptions (614) 383-5772
Direct Sales Jud Chappell (Manager), Julie Binion, Marty Click, Bob Richardson, Brett Setter
Corporate Sales Patti Harris (Manager), Angie Calandro, Kandace Elmore, Jeff Greer, Joanna Hayden, Brian Kosley, Laura Patterson, Sheri Smith
Marketing Mary Campana, Von Daniel, Robert Gregory, Gayle Klancnik, Marcia Stoesz, Hugh Murphy, Dawn Sturgeon
New Media Omar Mediano (Manager), Cara Carmichael, Amy Durrett, Tom Layberger, John Marshall, Jay Zwerner
Subscriptions Jenifer Grellhesl, Christine Seibert
Information Services Airey Baringer (Senior Manager), Dana Alecknavage, Randall Calvert, Chris Hellem
Fulfillment Mike Moss (Manager), Albert Chavez, Gean Paul Figari, Mark Hartley, Randy Mosty, John Randall, Bryan Winstead
Facilities Jim Tereschuk (Manager), Bob Brown

Accounting Teri McGahey (Manager), Susan Catka, Sherry Monday
Operations Mary Gregory (Manager), Loretta Gibbs, Rosanna Gonzalez-Oleachea, Julie Grove, Stanley Lira, Mila Morante, Stacy Olivieri, Wendy Pallugna
Human Resources Jane Ann Layton (Manager), Kaye Ball, Carol Fowler, Doree Tate

Editorial Correspondence: Unsolicited manuscripts should be addressed to: Editorial Dept., Beckett Publications, 15850 Dallas Parkway, Dallas, Texas 75248.
All submissions, including letters to the editor, are subject to editing for style and content. The opinions expressed in bylined articles are those of the author. They are not necessarily those of the publisher or this publication.

Unsolicited Materials: Unsolicited manuscripts, artworks, photos and other materials will be reviewed as time permits. Only those materials accompanied by an SASE with sufficient postage will be returned. Beckett Publications cannot be held responsible for unsolicited materials.

Dealer Accounts Correspondence: All correspondence regarding consignment sales of Beckett Products should be addressed to: Dealer Accounts, 15850 Dallas Parkway, Dallas, Texas 75248.

World Wide Web Home Page: http://www.beckett.com

The Man

Packers legend Bart Starr believes Brett Favre has the right stuff to keep Green Bay on top

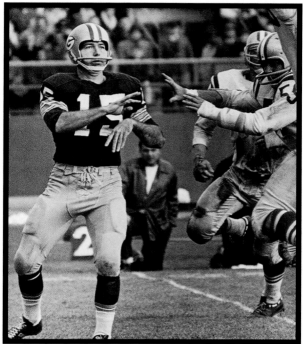

I have had the opportunity to speak with Brett Favre several times, and I am always impressed with him. He has a great work ethic. And there again is that leadership factor.

I have yet to see over the years another quarterback like Brett. When I was a rookie with the Packers, Tobin Rote was the quarterback. He wasn't playing on great teams, but I learned a lot from Tobin Rote about toughness and leadership. Brett embodies those qualities.

He's well above any parallel with me. That young man is in orbit. I was an overachiever, and I was blessed by playing on great teams with great players. Brett can throw the ball farther falling down than I could with a running start. And Brett's nature as a blue-collar player is perfect for Green Bay.

His competitiveness, his courage, his toughness . . . You could put him in Siberia and he'd play the same way.

I think that [Brett] also has benefited from great coaching. I have tremendous respect for Mike Holmgren and his coaching staff. There was no question when Brett came into the league he had that tremendously strong arm. I don't want to say that he was a thrower, because that's not fair to him, but it bordered on that. There's a huge difference between a thrower and a passer. But working diligently with Mike, working with that system, I think that he has become a superb passer. That's the transition that was made. Brett working with Coach Holmgren's system is simply a great fit.

Coach Lombardi would have loved Brett Favre. He truly leads by example. He is so tough and so courageous. He is a great leader. [Brett] is absolutely the quarterback to lead Green Bay. . . . I think its success is a great thing for Green Bay, a great thing for all the die-hard football fans out there.

Bart Starr earned legendary status as quarterback of the Vince Lombardi-era Green Bay Packers. Between 1961 and 1967, Starr led the Packers to five NFL championships and won the MVP trophy in Super Bowls I and II.

BY BART STARR

(AS TOLD TO MICHAEL BAUMAN)

Michael Bauman covers the Packers for the Milwaukee Journal Sentinel.

TABLE OF

AL MESSERSCHMIDT

CONTENTS

Front cover photo
Courtesy of Pinnacle Brands Inc.

Back cover photo by
Doug Pensinger / AllSport USA

Leadership

*During his five seasons with Brett Favre
in Green Bay, tight end Mark Chmura has
watched his good friend earn his standing
as the undisputed leader of the Pack*

Brett Favre and I have been
here five years, and during that time, I've seen him gradually progress into
the leader of our team. Each year, he has taken on more and more responsibility. Last year the offense was his. He runs the show out there. He tells
guys what he wants done. He does all the talking out there.

In the Super Bowl when we were behind 14-10 in the first quarter to the
Patriots, he showed no sense of panic and nobody else on the team showed
any panic. When most teams get into that situation, like Buffalo for example, they tend to fall apart. I think in one of the Bills' Super Bowl games
(one of four losses) they were actually up. Then they fell behind and just

BY MARK CHMURA AS TOLD TO TODD KORTH

'He runs the show out there. He tells guys what he wants done. He does all the talking out there.'

'Like I said, he's our Michael Jordan.

When the chips are down,

everybody looks to Brett.'

went into the tank. That's not the case with this team, and I think a lot of it is because of Brett. He's so confident in what he does.

When we did fall behind New England, we went out for the next series, and he just said, "Let's get it done." Guys just play off of his confidence. He's so confident in what he does. He's the best in the league, and he knows he's the best in the league. I think guys respect that.

In crunch time everybody looks to Brett. He's kind of like Michael Jordan, and everyone respects him because he is the top guy. I can't think of too many quarterbacks in this league who actually like to get into

scuffles with the other team. If there's ever a problem, Brett is one of the first guys over there to get involved, where most quarterbacks are running to the sideline because they don't want to get hurt. He might be the toughest quarterback to ever play this game, and guys respect that.

Two years ago he really hurt his ankle in a loss to the Minnesota Vikings in the Metrodome. It was badly sprained and he was on crutches on Thursday, three days before our next game against Chicago, and we weren't sure whether he was going to play. No one did (know) until he ran out of the tunnel and high-stepped

his way onto the field.

That's how he gets respect from all of us. I wouldn't have expected him to play that game. He didn't have to play the game. But he felt he was letting us down if he didn't. Then he went out and threw five touchdown passes and we won, 35-28. We lost only one of our next six games, and we went on to win the (1995) Central Division title for like the first time in 23 years (the first outright division title since 1972, not counting the crown during

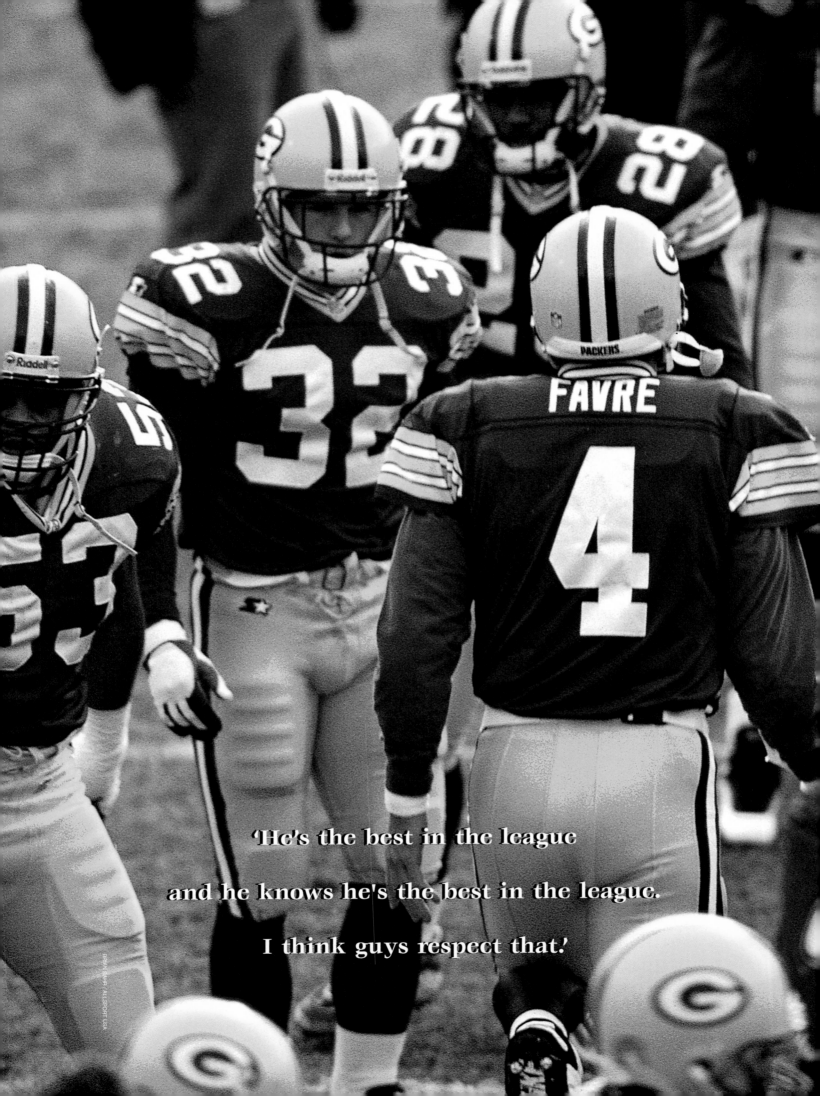

'He's the best in the league

and he knows he's the best in the league.

I think guys respect that.'

the strike-shortened 1982 campaign).

Like I said, he's our Michael Jordan. When the chips are down, everybody looks to Brett. Five years ago, he was pretty much just dropping back and winging it. Now he's such a smart player, he knows what everybody should be doing on the field. Everybody looks to him at crunch time, and he produces every time he's put into that situation.

It was a different kind of crunch time for him last year when he publicly admitted his addiction to painkillers. Not too many

people can do that, especially people in his position. He's in the national spotlight. To come out and admit that you have a problem takes a lot of courage. Most people would try to hide it in some sort of way, but he was man enough to come out, admit it and deal with it. Not only deal with it but put it behind him and go out and lead this team to a world championship. He just knew he needed help. He knows what he did was wrong, and now he's back to the same old Brett.

From the time that he was traded by Atlanta to Green Bay in 1992, I feel

The leader of the Pack has that unique ability to connect with teammates off and on the field.

that he has really matured. Each year he has matured a little more. We were pretty wild the first couple of years here. We liked to go out and have a good time, but in the last couple of years, Brett has really slowed down. He got married last year, so we enjoy doing other things now. Four or five years ago, we loved to go out. Now we all just get together and go play golf, or go watch a movie, or go to dinner or

PATS 21   0   BALL   0:00
                T.O.L. DOWN
PACKERS 35 <   1   TO GO   QTR 4

The Packers trailed early in Super Bowl XXXI, but with Favre on the job, they believed they ultimately would prevail.

something like that.

While he's matured in one area, he has declined in another. He's always playing jokes, whether it's in the locker room or away from it. He just got me a couple of months ago. He put some Red Hot in my underwear before I went out to dinner. The stuff didn't hit me until about halfway through the dinner, and I was just sitting there sweating. It was a formal dinner, too. I just had to sweat my way through it. That was what killed me. I couldn't leave. It's an old trick but a goodie. **F**

Throughout the last five years, tight end Mark Chmura and Brett Favre have become the best of friends.

"We see each other quite a bit year round. We play a lot of golf," Chmura says.

As their friendship and golf games have blossomed, so has their production on the football field. Favre was named the league's Most Valuable Player the last two

The Packers gladly follow
Favre into battle because
they know he never backs
down from a fight.

'From the time he was

first traded by Atlanta to

Green Bay in 1992, I feel

that he has matured.'

Since Favre, Chmura and Frank Winters joined the Pack in '92, they haven't finished below 9-7.

seasons, while Chmura had a breakthrough season in 1995 by catching 54 passes for 679 yards and pacing all tight ends with seven touchdowns.

His peers rewarded him by naming him to the NFC Pro Bowl squad.

Fortune smiled on Mark before his charmed season. He was expected to play behind All-Pro tight end Keith Jackson in '95, but when Jackson held out of training camp and the first six games of the season, Chmura made the most of the opportunity. Even when Jackson ended his 91-day holdout, Mark remained the starting tight end.

Last year, Chmura split time with Jackson, but Mark missed three games during the middle of the season after suffering a severely sprained left arch Nov. 10 against Kansas City. He returned to catch a total of 10 passes in the Packers' final three regular season games and finished the season with 28 catches for 370

Brett's wedding in the summer of '96 featured a peck from the flower girl and kicked off a super year for the field general.

yards. He added three more receptions in the playoffs and scored a two-point conversion in Green Bay's 35-21 Super Bowl XXXI victory over the Patriots.

The Packers selected the Boston College first-team All-American in the sixth round of the 1992 draft, a banner off-season highlight-ed by the deal with Atlanta for Favre and the drafting of

Chmura, wide receiver Robert Brooks and running back Edgar Bennett. Mark suffered a back injury that landed him on the injured reserve list his rookie year. He contemplated quitting football at the time, but head coach Mike Holmgren managed to convince him to stay.

In 1993, he backed up Jackie Harris and Ed West and caught just two passes. He started the final four games of the 1994 season and both of Green Bay's ensuing playoff games when West went down with an

ankle injury, and for the year, Mark finished with 14 catches.

Thanks to his hard work and determination, Mark received a three-year, $4.8 million contract in February 1996. This season, Chmura will be the main man at tight end. Jackson retired from football in March, leav-ing Chmura as the club's leader at that position.

"[Playing full time] is something I've done before and can handle," Chmura says.

Todd Korth is the editor of Packer Report.

Competitiveness

Much of Brett Favre's refuse-to-lose attitude comes from father Irv, who had to balance his role as dad with the role of head coach during Brett's youth

I don't remember ever having a doubt in my mind that Brett was competitive. He's always played aggressive — played smart. He was a sort of smart, mean type kid when it came to sports and such. He'd hit hard and throw hard. Everything about him was hard.

You could tell just by watching him grow up that he was aggressive. He couldn't stand to come in second — ever. If Brett had a bad game, came in second, you knew you were going to have to hear about it. He always wanted to be No. 1 in everything. And he never really failed very much.

Even in about fifth grade, when he was just playing peewee football,

BY IRV FAVRE AS TOLD TO MONIQUE HARRISON

Many of Brett's proudest moments as a professional football player have been witnessed by his dad, who also got an up-close view of his son's accomplishments as a youth on the baseball diamond.

I could tell he had the aggression he needed. Of course, that didn't really surprise me. I think all three of my boys had that.

I never was really surprised by it. I didn't think it was anything unusual. Through the years, I saw a lot of kids that had that same aggression. It's obvious where most of them get it from.

I mean, Brett heard it from me coaching. You could go out and say it was just a game, that second place was OK sometimes, but that's not really true. You don't go out

there to come in second. Heck, you go out there to win.

And kids know that, whether you ever say it or not. I think, in America, having aggressive, competitive players is what's expected. Kids don't have to be told that. The good ones just live up to it.

I coached Brett in high school — coached all three of my sons. And, of course, I watched them all play in peewee, junior high and all that. I could tell Brett stood above the rest even when he was young. I could tell he was probably going to be better than most in high school.

I'm not going to sit here and say he was a great athlete at a young age, because he wasn't. He had skill and he was big for his age, but not exceptional. But I could tell that his being competi-

tive could make the difference.

Competitiveness alone won't win games, but when someone has some skill and then has competitiveness, they have a chance to be good. I knew Brett had a chance. I just didn't know what he would do with it.

I've had people ask me when I realized Brett was pro material, and the answer to that might be never. I mean, I was around him every day. I got used to his ability, and I think I underestimated him in some ways. I think a lot of people underestimated him back then. Of course, he had a lot to learn coming out of high school. Everyone does.

Brett really impressed me when he went in at quarterback (for USM) against Tulane when he was only 17 and in his freshman year. He

'Competitiveness alone won't win games, but when someone has some skill and then has competitiveness, they have a chance to be good. I knew Brett had a chance. I just did not know what he would do with it.'

led the team to victory and showed some real leadership ability during that game.

It's hard to get the kind of respect you need from your team to win a game when you are just 17 and you are playing with guys who are 22 or 23. They had to have some respect for him to respond like they did. If you were going to notice Brett, it was probably going to be after that game.

Brett was never lazy, but then practicing was never a problem with any of my kids. They liked to practice.

We tried to make practice fun and interesting. They played together a lot at home, and I think each one of those three wanted to be better than the rest. But I

Not surprisingly, the Favre men grew up in a competitive household. Brett, along with father Irv and brothers Scott and Jeff, all played sports together in their younger years.

never heard any of them say, "I'm better than you," or "I'm going to beat you," or anything like that. With brothers, you expect that to be there. But they just got out in the yard and played together and helped each other. Brett and our oldest (Scott) hung out together a lot. They supported each other. They are very close.

Some people have said Brett grew up with advantages, me being his coach. But Brett was a go-getter. He's the type of guy that if you say he can't do it, he'll show you you're wrong.

It goes back to his competitive nature. Any athlete has to work hard to get anywhere, and Brett has done that for a long time. That separates the good from the not-so-good, especially in college. You have to work hard studying the game. You have to work in the off-season. You have to work in the weight program.

I think Brett did those

things. He worked hard to be good in practice, and that's what got him in the game when he was young. Brett worked hard, and all the rest fell in place.

He had mononucleosis during his sophomore year (at USM) and wasn't able to play. That probably set him back a little as far as experience goes. But he came back and everything fell into place again. I don't think he's had much to overcome, nothing more than most people, anyway. We all have something to overcome. Brett has handled his well. I'm proud of him — proud of all of them.

One thing he has had to learn — and maybe this is part of his competitive nature — is that he doesn't have to be a strong man with the football in his hand. He's been known as a gunslinger, someone who throws the football as hard as he can.

While he was at USM, the coaches taught him to be more polished. He got some

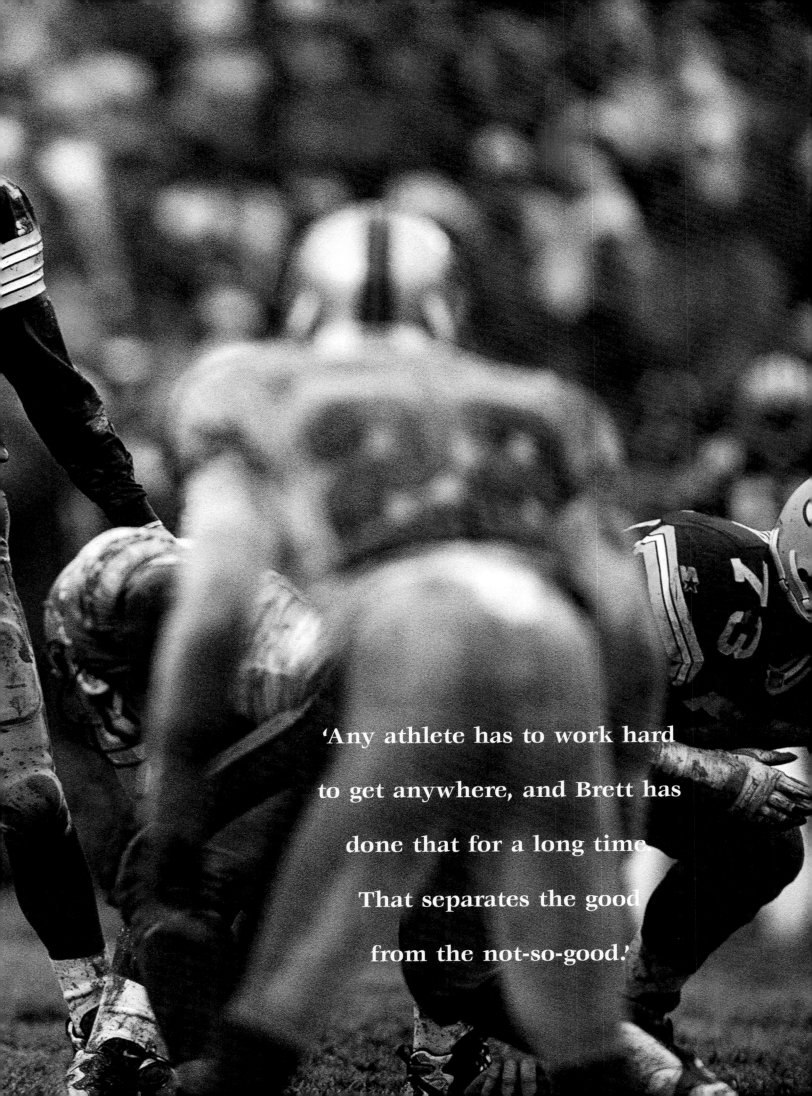

'Any athlete has to work hard
to get anywhere, and Brett has
done that for a long time.
That separates the good
from the not-so-good.'

'I could tell Brett stood above

the rest, even when he was young.

I could tell he was probably

going to be better than most

in high school.'

'You could go out and say it was just a game, that second place was OK sometimes, but that's not really true. You don't go out there to come in second. Heck, you go out there to win.'

good coaching there, and that helped prepare him.

Brett's a lot more polished now. He's still competitive, still strong, but he has learned a little finesse. His skills are stronger. He's always been a smart player, but now he's even smarter because he doesn't rely on strength quite as much. **F**

Irv Favre knows a little something about his son's willingness to compete. Irv coached Brett during his high school football years and also served as his coach during summer league baseball.

Irv, now 52, coached football at Hancock Attendance Center in Kiln, Miss., for 24 years and spent a total of 29 years coaching high school sports. He retired three years ago to farm about 100 acres in Kiln — including 52 of his own and the adjoining 44 purchased by Brett to launch an angus farm.

"I raise his black angus cattle now," Irv explains. "I don't know a whole lot about those cows, but I'm learning. If nothing else, I have a new respect for farmers.

"It's hard work, but I

Brett's competitive nature has helped him become a more complete quarterback, doing whatever it takes to help the team win, whether it's by the ground or through the air.

enjoy it. I'm an outside guy — someone who likes to cut grass and things like that."

When the former coach is not farming, he often can be found watching live or televised sports. "Of course, Green Bay is my favorite team at the moment," he says. "I catch a lot of airplanes to watch that boy of mine play. I love watching

Despite injuries to many
of his favorite targets last
season, Brett remained
focused on the job at
hand: bringing Green Bay
its first championship in
29 years.

Brett Favre was much more than a spectator during last season's Super Bowl run. His enthusiasm lifted his teammates, and his competitive nature rubbed off on everyone around.

any sports.

"During the season, I try to get my work [on the farm] done during the week so I can travel on weekends."

The Favres' oldest son, Scott, 30, runs Brett's prop-

erty management company in Diamondhead, Miss. Son Jeff, 23, recently moved to Milwaukee to work for a bank, where he handles mutual funds. The Favres' youngest child, daughter Brandy, is 20 and is a sophomore at the University of Southern Mississippi.

Monique Harrison is a graduate of the University of Southern Mississippi and currently works as a reporter for the Northeast Mississippi Daily Journal.

Family Loyalty

After the Little League and peewee football games were over, Bonita Favre used to gather her family around the dinner table and wonder if they could talk about anything other than sports

Everyone around here pretty much knew we were a close-knit bunch of people. People knew that everything we did — literally everything — seemed to revolve around sports and our love of sports. We literally lived from season to season, and our lives were ruled by what season it was.

The kids played everything. Irv coached summer league (baseball), so all summer, he was busy doing that, and, of course, he coached at the school, too. And while he was doing that, I was usually the one who had to get everyone else to their summer baseball games. They all played ball and loved it. Of course, like most kids in a family, they were never on the

BY BONITA FAVRE AS TOLD TO MONIQUE HARRISON

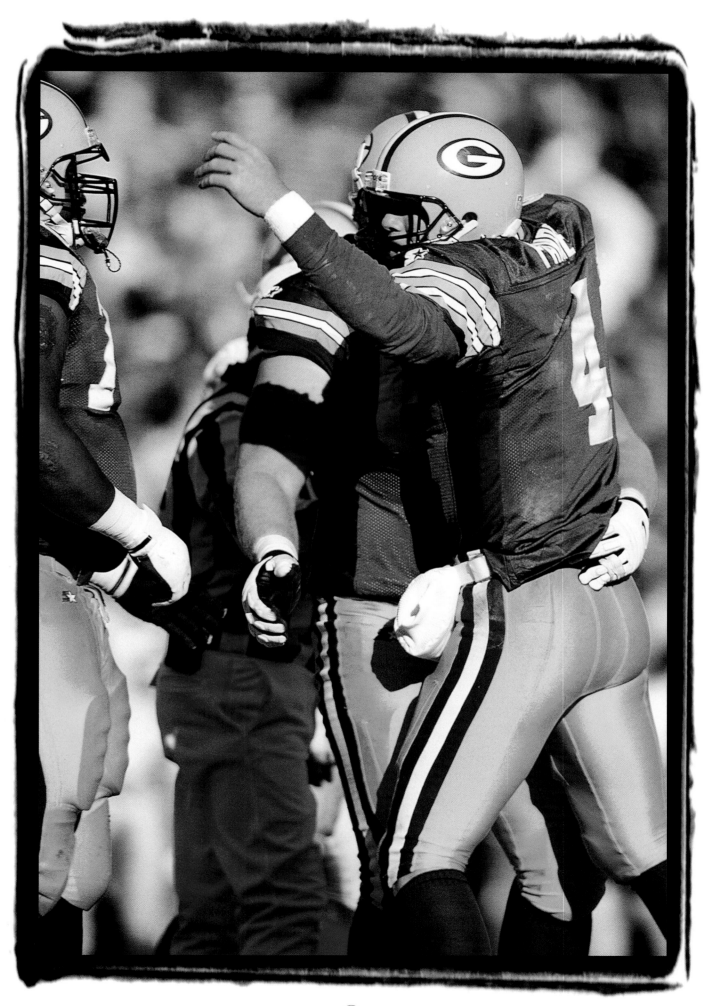

same team. So I was always trying to run them from one game or practice to another.

Sometimes, the games or practices would be going on in different places at one time, so I'd have to get someone else — a family friend or someone — to get them where they needed to be. Sometimes we would pass each other on the road out here. But one way or another, they got there.

We didn't really have family vacations. We didn't have the time for that — or the money. Usually, our family vacation was when my

husband's (summer league boys) team had to go to some kind of state tournament or something. That was usually somewhere in North Mississippi, so the whole family would load up in the van and ride up for that. Our summer was nothing but sports — that was all we had time for. But the kids were happy that way, and they got to spend time together when we would go for those tournaments.

Looking back now that I have time, I don't know how we did it all. But at the time, I just did it all. When you

Sports were a big part of the lives of Brett and brothers Scott and Jeff. No question which pro team the family roots for now — Brett's Green Bay Packers.

are that busy living, you don't think about it — don't think about if any of your children will go pro or even play well in college. You just do it, and you live life from season to season.

Of all my children, I always said that Brett was the one who would be the most likely to be an only child or the one that would

Favre might not have minded if he had been an only child, but he still was close with each of his brothers. As children, oldest brother Scott and youngest brother Jeff were just as active in a variety of sports as Brett.

like to be an only child. He loved his brothers and sister, I guess, and he was really close to our oldest boy, Scott. But he still probably would have really liked to have been the only one we had. He was kind of selfish, and sometimes he got him-

self into trouble for that. He liked to have his own cup and his own food. He didn't like for anyone to eat or drink after him. If they did, he wouldn't finish it. He was funny that way. Sometimes, the boys argued about their room. The three of them all shared a room. It had three closets — dormitory style I guess is what you would call it. Brett was the one who insisted he have his own bed. He just didn't like to share. But that's how kids are — each one of them in a family has their own person-ality. Brett had the personali-

ty of an only child.

I didn't really know it at the time, because they didn't ever tell me, but Brett was sort of the terror in the fami-ly. When I wasn't around, he was always pulling some kind of stunt — playing jokes on his brothers or something. Not too long ago I found out he used to tie poor Jeff up in his bed. He was always into something, that Brett.

All of the kids had a lot of friends growing up, and those friends were usually around here. They didn't have a bowling alley or any-

'. . . You don't think about it — don't think about

if any of your children will go pro or even

play well in college. You just do it and

live from season to season.'

'Brett was sort of the terror in the family. When I wasn't around, he was always pulling some kind of stunt.'

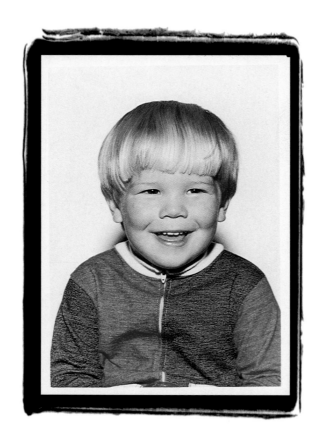

thing like that in Kiln. There's not much for kids to do. So the kids would all come out here because we have so much space (outdoors). There's a big field and the kids would get out there and play ball and things.

There would be a crowd of them out there, in the field and in the woods. About 17 years ago, we built a swimming pool. You can just bet we had lots of kids around after that happened! This was sort of the place for everyone to be, and we had

some friends that lived around here who had four children. We did some things together with them, and that was a lot of fun. But you can get the idea. It was all family time. We did things together. It's the way we were.

Anyone can figure that it's not as easy for Brett now to spend that kind of time with his family. I think he'd like to raise his daughter in some of the same ways we raised him. He's on the road so much. Brittany (Brett's 8-year-old daughter) goes to one school during football

Always the prankster, young Brett terrorized his brothers long before casting his playful eye on NFL defensive backs.

season and then moves down here. It's hard for her sometimes. She's around adults a lot. One year, we kept her while (Brett's wife and Brittany's mom Deanna) was finishing up school. Sometimes, she travels with Brett. She goes down to Disney World every year for the Quarterback Challenge. I think that's almost gotten

old to her. She travels so much, things that would be exciting for other children are just no big deal for her.

But she likes sports — she's taking golf lessons and horse riding lessons right now. Maybe that's something she and Brett can do together. I've always thought she'd either love sports or hate them because she's been around them so much already.

That's how it was with my kids. Since their dad was a coach, that was almost all they heard growing up. They would hear it at practice, and hear it driving home from practice. Sometimes at the dinner table, I would just ask if we could go through a single meal without talking about some sport. But, you know, I don't know if we ever really did. But that's OK, because they loved it, and I did, too. They had the ability to play, and that helped. But it was more than that. They were all committed to it. They would run up and down this road out here to get in shape. They watched what they ate and

Favre's family was always there for him, including hanging around for one of the biggest days of young Brett's life — the NFL draft. The Falcons may have called on that day, but Brett eventually ended up in Green Bay.

how much they ate. It was a way of life for them — sports were certainly what this family was about. **F**

Bonita Favre, 51, dedicated about 25 years of her life to shuttling her four

'Sometimes at the dinner table,

I would just ask if we could go through

a single meal without talking about

some sport. But that's OK, because they

loved it, and I did, too.'

After the Packers' victory in Super Bowl XXXI, Favre and his teammates basked in the glow of an NFL championship. Later, he and wife Deanna toured the New Orleans streets.

children to countless junior high, high school and recreational league football and baseball games, not to mention church activities and social outings. The former special education teacher also headed up the Athletic Booster Club at Hancock Attendance Center, where her husband coached and her four children attended school in Kiln, Miss.

She was known at the school for being a top-rate money-raiser, despite living in a rural area where money for junior high and high school athletics was often hard to come by.

Bonita is now retired from teaching but still finds herself devoting a large amount of her time to the booming career of son Brett. She currently handles payroll and other activities for his publicity agency. She also spends time coordinating the activities of her 79-year-old mother.

"I have a magnet on my refrigerator that says, 'Do you know where your mother is?' " Bonita says. "And the truth is, there are a lot of times when I honestly don't.

"We call her a world traveler. But I'm glad I can see her enjoying herself, and I'm glad I'm still enjoying myself. I think I' am very fortunate."

Monique Harrison is a graduate of the University of Southern Mississippi and currently works as a reporter for the Northeast Mississippi Daily Journal.

Overcoming Odds

While many colleges liked Favre as a defensive back, USM head coach Curley Hallman gave Brett a chance on offense. Four years and 29 wins later, it appeared Curley made the right choice.

It's a rare situation to play a freshman. A lot of times people put freshmen in situations because they don't have anyone else. Going back to Brett's freshman season, his first start was against us at Texas A&M, and we were playing in Jackson. I had no idea then that in two or three months I'd be the head coach at Southern Mississippi.

We'd played our first two games, and we were awfully good defensively. We'd gotten after the kid from Washington (quarterback Chris Chandler), who was a preseason Heisman candidate, pretty good. Our defense was called the Wrecking Crew, and the name fit. We wrecked that young man.

So I'm sitting there when we're getting ready to play Southern Miss,

BY CURLEY HALLMAN AS TOLD TO PARRISH ALFORD

and this freshman's getting his first game to start. I'm thinking he's got to be in awe.

The biggest thing I remember from that game is walking down on the sidelines before the game trying to get a little bit on his snap count and rhythm and all that. I remember thinking he's got a little poise, about a half-cocky kind of kid, walking there pigeon-toed.

To make a long story short, it was a dogfight. We never sacked him. It was tied at halftime and we reeled off two long runs in the second half and beat them by 13 points. They had a chance to beat us, and we were a great defensive football team. I remember after the game in our locker room, Coach (Jackie) Sherrill saying, "That kid's gonna be a great quarterback."

(USM went 6-5 that year. The next season, Hallman's first as the Golden Eagles' head coach, the sophomore

Good times, bad times — Favre has had his share. In college, he was injured in a car wreck that required the removal of nearly 3 feet of his intestines.

quarterback led his team to a 10-2 record and a win over UTEP in the Independence Bowl. During Brett's junior campaign, USM upset Florida State, 30-26, on the road to start the 1989 season. The Golden Eagles also beat Louisville, 16-10, when

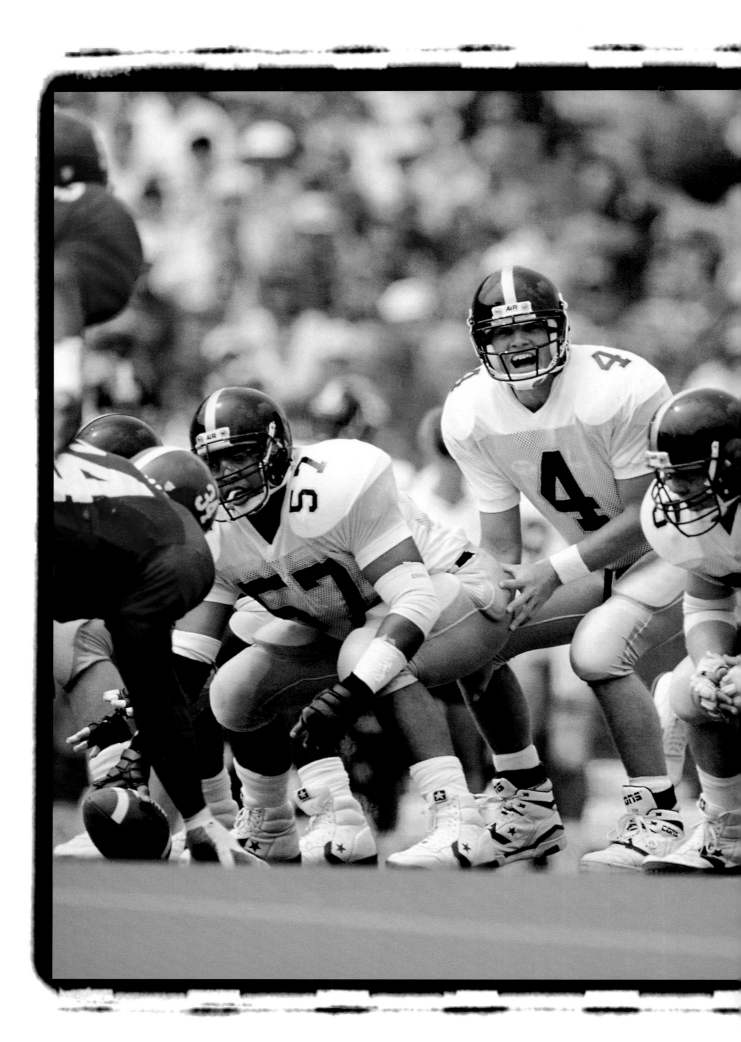

'I'm sitting there when we're getting ready to play Southern Miss, and this young freshman's getting his first game to start. I'm thinking he's got to be in awe. . . . I remember after the game in our locker room, Coach [Jackie] Sherrill saying, "That kid's gonna be a great quarterback."'

Even in high school, Brett (No. 10, bottom right) had to fight hard for recognition. Most colleges were interested in his skills as a defensive back, but USM took a chance on Favre at QB. And now, even though the two-time NFL MVP has made quite a name for himself in Green Bay, the people of Kiln, Miss., haven't forgotten their hometown hero.

'[During the game] he took a shot on their sideline, and I just said, "Wow, that might have done it." I was anxious to see him get off the ground and respond in the way that Brett always responded.... He looked at me and gave me a nod to say, "I'm fine." '

Favre threw a 60-yard touchdown pass on the last play.)

But then, before Brett's senior season, he was involved in the car wreck. He had some internal injuries and he had surgery in August.

One month after he underwent surgery, he started when we beat Alabama (who was ranked No. 13 at the time), 27-24. We also won that season at 15th-ranked Auburn, 13-12. We went 8-3 and we could have been called Alabama state champions.

He goes out there in the Alabama game and doesn't have a great game, but his presence in the huddle, his presence under the center, was a big plus for our team.

With Favre behind center, USM made victories over national powers like Auburn, Florida State and Alabama look as routine as a snap count.

I never made a decision until Friday morning that I was even going to play him. Of course that whole week he was like a little puppy dog, saying, "Coach, I'm fine."

We went through a process that week . . . a build-up. First, he had a walk-around on the field. The next progression was wearing a helmet and getting used to the heat and humidity; then in a couple days taking some snaps without a drop.

Then we let him get involved in some real low-key stuff, where he took a snap and just handed it off or threw a little dump pass.

It was a very slow build-up. I was not going to put him in a ballgame unless I knew he could protect himself. And we had blitz pick-up a couple of days that week, and he handled it. That was what I finally based my decision on. I announced to the team that

Brett would start, and it got them even more fired up and really raised their confidence level.

[During the game] he took a shot on their sideline, and I said, "Wow, that might have done it." I was anxious to see him get off the ground and respond in the way that Brett always responded. He finally did. You could just watch his body language as he got up and got on back. He looked over at me and gave me a nod and a hand to say, "I'm fine."

Our original plan was to rotate him. But he handled it. He wasn't 100 percent, but he was able to protect himself and perform. Alabama didn't think he was going to play. But one coach kept telling them he was going to play. I guess they had somebody watching us.

Later that year against Auburn, we were losing late in the game, and I remember Brett coming up on the sidelines and telling me,

"Coach, we're gonna win this thing." It's 12-0, and we're in the fourth quarter. Then he hits Michael Jackson to make it 12-7, and from that point on, there's not a guy on our team who doesn't think we're going to win the football game.

Brett was just an athlete. He'd see things around him. He'd feel things that he couldn't even see.

I have been around guys who had the intensity in them, and they all were excellent players, but they just didn't all have the other things to go with it. **F**

Fact: Life has obstacles. They can be minor bumps on the road to success or canyons in a wilderness of failure, and how you handle them defines who you are.

For Brett Favre, facing down the obstacles in life appeared to be as simple as dodging a pothole on the plentiful two-lane highways in south Mississippi — step, plant, cut and you *are back on track.*

Favre never strayed far from the track at the University of Southern Mississippi. He led the Golden Eagles to a come-from-behind win over Tulane in just the second

During his professional and college careers, Favre has often taken a lickin'. But through sheer grit and determination, and by staying focused on the job at hand, he's always been able to keep on tickin'.

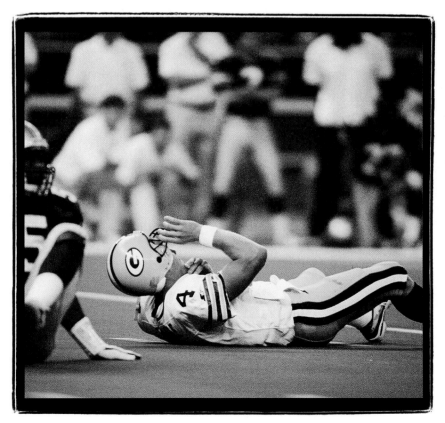

Interestingly enough, Brett, as Southern a boy as you will ever find, has thrived in cold weather. In his first 14 starts for games in which the temperature was 35 degrees or lower, Favre was 14-0, resulting in many a victory celebration.

'Brett was just an athlete. He'd

see things around him. He'd feel

things that he couldn't even see.'

'It's 12-0 [USM was losing to Auburn] and we're in the fourth quarter. Then he hits Michael Jackson to make it 12-7, and from that point on, there's not a guy on our team who doesn't think we're going to win the football game.'

game of his freshman season. Three years later, he was able to shake off the effects of a near-fatal car wreck that required the surgical removal of 30 inches of his damaged intestines just weeks before his senior season.

During his collegiate career, he led his team to upset wins over college football landlords such as Florida State, Alabama and Auburn.

All along, Brett knew that success loomed nearby. During his college career,

he led USM to 29 victories. Two of those wins came during ever-important bowl games. During his four seasons, he managed to set school records for passing yards (8,193), pass attempts (1,234), completions (656), passing percentage (53) and touchdowns (55) while throwing just 35 interceptions.

He was the MVP his senior year of both the All-American Bowl, in which the Golden Eagles lost, 31-27, to N.C. State, and the East-West Shrine game,

Early on, Favre would hang in the pocket too long. As he's matured, he's learned when to run, and when to throw it away.

the college all-star game featuring the nation's best seniors.

Curley Hallman and Favre climbed some mountains together for three years at Southern Mississippi.

Hallman, an assistant coach on two national championship teams, took over as head coach at USM

No matter the obstacle, Favre has shown a unique ability to pick himself up and move on, earning him the respect of teammates and coaches alike.

as Favre was hitting his prime as a sophomore.

Together they helped maintain a long-standing Southern Miss tradition of pulling off road upsets against premier college football programs.

The Northport, Ala., native was 23-11 as the head coach at USM from 1988 to 1990.

He left Hattiesburg,

Miss., for LSU in the fall of '90 and saw his Tiger teams approach the corner but never turn it. He resigned after the 1994 season with a 16-28 record.

He was the secondary coach at Texas A&M prior to accepting the USM job. It was actually during his days at Texas A&M that Hallman first saw Favre, who was starting as a freshman when USM played the Aggies in Jackson, Miss.

Hudson "Curley" Hallman, a former All-Southwest Conference defensive back at Texas A&M, is now in his second

season as the secondary coach at Alabama. It's the same position he held on Paul "Bear" Bryant's 1973 SEC and national championship team. Hallman was also an assistant on Danny Ford's national championship team at Clemson in 1981.

The former head coach of a major college football program now just enjoys being home in Northport.

***Parrish Alford covered USM when Favre was quarterback. Alford now covers Mississippi State for the* Northeast. Mississippi Daily Journal.**

Small-Town Hero

A lifelong Packers fan, the mayor of
Green Bay appreciates Brett Favre as much
for his down-home values as his MVP talent

Let's say everyone knew Brett Favre had the talent to be the league's Most Valuable Player two straight seasons. Then they took all of his talent and leadership abilities and looked at all 30 teams in the National Football League and asked, "Now where is it that his talent and his personality are going to flourish and where is he going to get the most out of his potential?" They would have to pick Green Bay.

He's not a guy looking for the glitz of a Los Angeles or New York. He's not a guy who is going to fit in with the moral fiber of a Dallas. He's a guy who is happy to be part of a winning squad, and he wants to do as much

BY MAYOR PAUL F. JADIN AS TOLD TO TODD KORTH

as he can to make his team a winner. He comes from a blue-collar background that many of the people in Green Bay have come from. So, he's one of us.

I'm sure his upbringing was very similar to the upbringing of people in this area. Green Bay has about 100,000 residents in a county of roughly 200,000 people. Many Green Bay natives have received an upbringing

that includes a moral foundation, a focus and an appreciation of who you are. It's evident that Brett received that same type of upbringing in Kiln, Miss.

Brett has received many awards, especially in the last two years, but his success hasn't changed who he really is. Brett is from a small town. If you look around northeastern Wisconsin, there are Kilns all over the place. I grew up in one —

If kids are searching for positive role models, Mayor Jadin suggests the hard-working, fun-loving leader of the Pack.

Kewaunee. Kewaunee and Kiln are probably not too different. It's pretty small, so even though Kiln and Green Bay are about 1,100 miles apart, the two areas feature small-town charm and a football superstar in Brett Favre.

Green Bay's fans flock to Favre because he's a superstar on a championship team and because he's truly one of them.

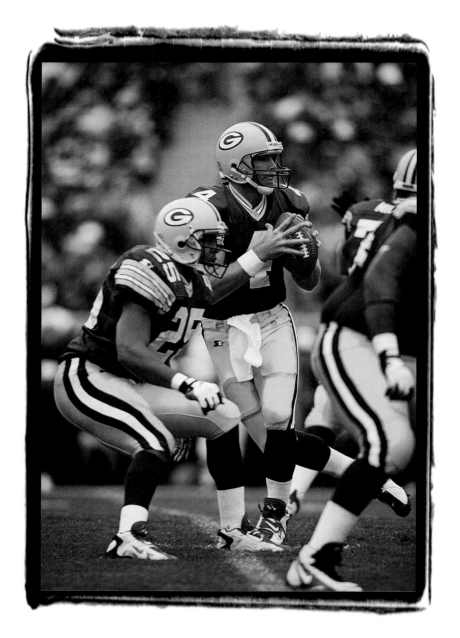

'[Brett's] a guy who is
happy to be part of a
winning squad, and he wants
to do as much as he can to
make his team a winner.'

'[Brett's] not a guy looking
for the glitz of a
Los Angeles or New York.'

With his surge in popularity in the last couple of years, I think he still can be pretty comfortable getting out in public in Kiln and in Green Bay. I know in Green Bay he is the type of person who relates well to the 22-year-old college student or the 30-year-old mill worker. That speaks well for his ego.

I think he's been comfortable here because, again, Kiln and Green Bay are very similar in ways, yet Green Bay offers something different for everyone. We're a community that can provide culture. There are first-class museums, historical sites, the performing arts, parks, private and public schools,

colleges and natural resources that are second to none.

The most significant thing Brett offers Green Bay is the attitude that money and success are not changing him, and that he has a work ethic very similar to what we pride ourselves in around here. He's going to get the job done whatever it takes.

He has shown that since he first came to Green Bay in 1992 and especially the last two years. He had a vision for the Packers, and he had personal goals. He knew he had to work through pain and adversity to achieve those things.

There's something to be

Beneath the uniform, the wealth and the awards, the kid from Kiln, Miss., isn't any different from the youth of Green Bay.

said for Green Bay's role in that. I think, to some extent, we keep him grounded. He could be influenced by other teammates or by the glitz that other communities have to offer, but I think that's something that Mike Holmgren should be given credit for doing. Mike knows how people need to act in Green Bay versus how they may be able to act in Los Angeles. I think he does a wonderful job of keeping his players focused. Yet at the

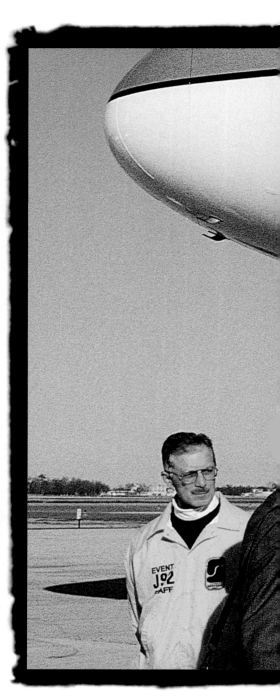

VERNON J. BIEVER (LEFT & ABOVE)

same time they don't have to sacrifice their personality. Brett's personality is a good fit here, and Mike makes sure that it stays a good fit.

I am personally and foremost a Packer fan. I've been a Packer fan all of my life, but I don't go out of my way to call the players and invite them to events in Green Bay, or anything like that. When I saw the opportunity for the Packers to have a special season last year, I didn't want to call Brett and

say, "Hey, I've got a committee for you to sit on, or I've got a project that I want you to help me with."

I want to make sure that he — as well as others associated with the Packers — has as few distractions as possible. I've met Reggie White and a few other players, but not because I've gone out of my way to get them involved in things. I'm happy that the private sector has that opportunity. I know Brett is involved in

Air Favre is flying high as the NFL's premier signal caller, but his roots remain in the rich values of small-town America. Turns out Green Bay isn't that different from Kiln, Miss.

the Boys and Girls Clubs of Green Bay and Robert Brooks has been involved with Special Olympics. I love to see that because those are a few of the ways that players can interact with the community in a

positive way.

I've been a Packer fan ever since I was 12 years old. I remember the Ice Bowl well and the Glory Years of the 1960s. Despite the fact that they're very different personalities, Brett Favre and Bart Starr have a lot in common. They both interact with the community in a positive way, and they appreciate their role as key members of the community.

No matter what happens around them, they never change. Bart might have a little more of a faith foundation than Brett might, but Brett is grounded in his personal value system.

Bart was always wearing his Christianity a little bit more, which certainly made him a prevalent role model. He still brings that to Green Bay today, even though he doesn't live here. Brett brings a different kind of non-football focus that I think kids can relate to.

Neither of them were cut out for Hollywood, necessarily. They were both Southern boys when they were drafted, and they both turned out to be fabulous quarterbacks. While they might come at you with a little different flair or personality, they both brought similar and wonderful things to the City of Green Bay.

Like Bart, Brett Favre is indeed a perfect fit for Green

Ever since Favre became the starting quarterback five years ago, the future once again has looked bright at Lambeau Field.

'I know [Brett's] the type of
person who relates well to the
22-year-old college student
or the 30-year-old mill worker.'

Bay and the Packers.   **F**

Having been reared in the small town of Kewaunee, Wis., Green Bay Mayor Paul F. Jadin can relate with Kiln, Miss., native Brett Favre.

In Favre, the mayor sees a quarterback who exemplifies what small-town values are all about.

Jadin, 42, also sees a two-time NFL MVP and marketable superstar who's comfortable playing in the league's smallest media

Since the Packers' commander in chief doesn't take himself too seriously, he isn't likely to let fame and fortune go to his head.

market, far removed from the glare radiating from the NFL's larger cities.

Jadin was elected mayor of Green Bay, population slightly more than 100,000, in April 1995. He was born in Green Bay and raised in Kewaunee, a small town east of Green Bay along the Lake Michigan shoreline. Prior to becoming mayor, Jadin served for seven years as the director of personnel and labor relations for the city, and he was chief negotiator in all collective bargaining cases.

Jadin received his bachelor's degree in political science from Northwestern University in 1977 and a master's in public adminis-

tration from Florida State in 1979. He is currently a member of three task forces for the U.S. Conference of Mayors, including the Sports Franchise Relocation Task Force. He also participates as an active member of the Wisconsin Alliance of Cities. A Green Bay Packers fan since he was a little boy, Jadin has followed the team through the Glory Years of the 1960s and its resurgence in the '90s, and the lean years of the 1970s and '80s.

"When the Packers won three straight championships [1965 NFL title and Super Bowls I and II], that was probably the highlight of my youth as a fan," Jadin recalls. "Obviously another

With plenty of time on his side, the 28-year-old Favre can look forward to many more victory celebrations before he retires.

highlight was this past season. Like everybody I suffered through the 1970s and '80s, and particularly those periods when the Packers were not only performing poorly on the field, but they were also bringing disrespect to the community."

Head coach Mike Holmgren, Favre and Reggie White, among others, initiated a new respect for the Packers and Green Bay.

"Brett Favre and the Green Bay Packers of the 1990s have brought a lot of positive attention to Green Bay," Jadin explains. "Brett certainly is a role model

and fun-loving guy who wants to go out and play ball and win. It's a relief from other athletes who seem to get so much of the attention these days. You saw it again when the Packers visited the White House on May 20. Brett was kind of rolling his eyes to President Clinton as Mike Holmgren was speaking, trying to keep things loose."

Jadin keeps an eye on the Packers by attending each home game. He often shares his seats in the stands or a luxury box with other politicians or developers to give them an up-close view of the positive, close-knit relationship between the Packers and the city of Green Bay.

Todd Korth is the editor of Packer Report.

Tradition

Hall of Fame linebacker Ray Nitschke says Brett Favre plays a little like the legendary Johnny Unitas and a whole lot like all the Packers' greats from the 1960s

I n the rich tradition of the Green Bay Packers, I feel there's definitely a place of honor for Brett Favre. He is certainly very deserving to be placed with prominence in the history of this football franchise.

Brett is a player who sets a great example for his teammates and for the way he goes about his performance. He simply exemplifies the character that you want in a football player. He's a championship type of person in the sense that he presents himself every game and plays with the intensity

BY RAY NITSCHKE AS TOLD TO TODD KORTH

In 1997, Favre & Co. rekindled memories of when Nitschke helped Lombardi's Packers claim the first Super Bowl trophy.

and the great mental toughness that I think you need to be a winner. Since he first arrived in 1992, he has played many games hurt, but he's got great pride. He does everything possible that it takes to win.

You know when you're watching the Packers that Brett is going to give it 100 percent every game. He's a credit to the franchise and a credit to his team and family. He's the kind of guy that former players like myself and all Packer fans can be proud to say that Brett Favre is our guy. He's our quarterback.

When Brett first started playing for the Packers, you could see that he was pretty tough. You could see his physical toughness on the field.

He's not afraid to get in an opponent's face. He took his lumps at first, but he hung in there and has gotten better with time.

You also could see from the start that he had all the physical attributes. It was just a matter of time for him. You could see from the first game on that he was going to be a fierce competitor, a guy who wants to do whatever it takes to win. He certainly gives everything he has in each game. You can't ask for anything more than that from a quarterback and a player.

He has led the Packers to

five straight winning seasons and four consecutive trips to the playoffs. The Packers have been in the NFC Championship Game the last two years and won their first Super Bowl in 29 years. He is the leader of the team just by his example. He's always fired up from the first play to the last play of game. He's always there, too. Brett has started 87 straight games, including the playoffs, which is by far the longest active streak by an NFL quarterback.

He's played through a lot of pain, and it's no secret that pain is prevalent in football. You've got to play through it. Quarterbacks are no different from linebackers or anybody else on a team, but Brett is one of pro football's special players. His

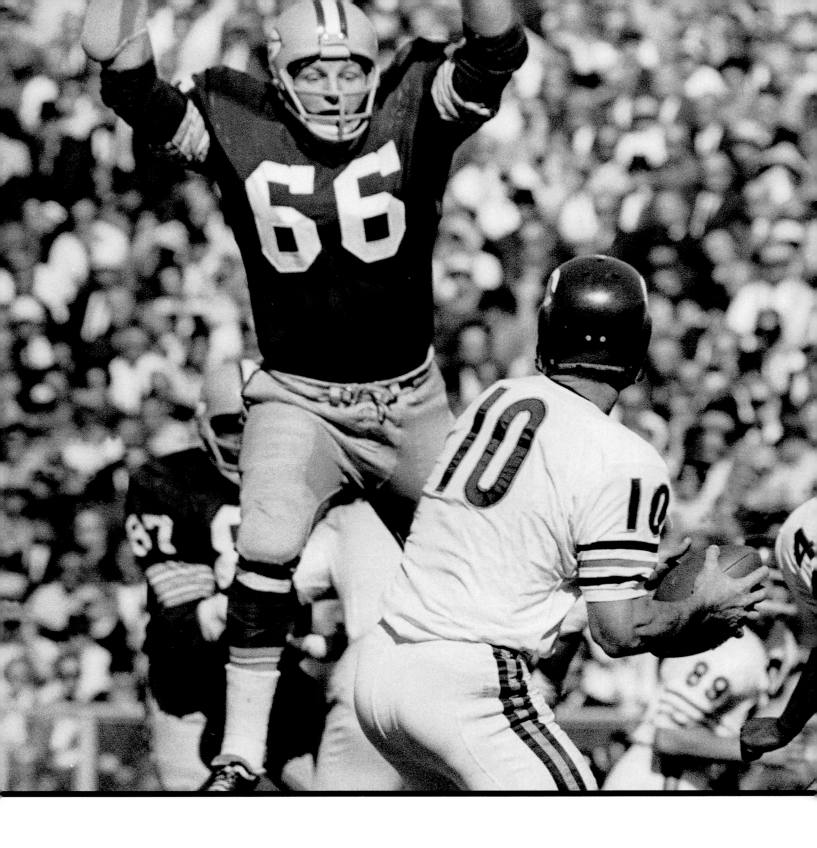

Had the hard-charging Nitschke played quarter-back, he would have attacked the position with the same aggressiveness as Favre.

public admission to a dependency on pain medication last year just showed that he's competitive and smart enough to take care of himself.

He spent time in a rehabilitation clinic, came back in great shape and led the Packers to a world championship. He not only helped himself as a football player, but as a human being.

A lot of people have compared Brett to Bart Starr. I feel that's unfair, but the similarities between him and Starr are that they're both poised and have excellent mental toughness.

To me, Bart Starr was mentally tough in the sense that he had control of his offense and he seemed to always rise to the occasion. I think Favre rises to the occa-

sion, too. That was quite evident last season. You never really saw any bad performances from Starr, and you don't from Favre, either.

Both are very consistent in the way they perform and certainly very similar in a sense that they want to win. Plus, they're both leaders. They're disciplined when learning the game. They're both students of the game. Bart never made many mistakes and always seemed to get better every year. Favre is the same way.

He's also a regular guy. Favre's the kind of person you immediately have to respect and admire. He's a solid young man. He loves the game and he treats people like you should treat people — with respect. He's a neat young man who pos-

The tradition continues: In 1995, Favre was the team's first consensus NFL MVP since 1966, the shining season of Bart Starr.

sesses a lot of physical ability to play football.

To me, he's got a lot of the traits of Johnny Unitas. He's physically and mentally tough. He's got great confidence and great control. He's got it all. And he loves the game. He loves to play.

Brett is the type of person and player who could fit in any era. He's a throwback type of player. Since he wants to do what he can to help his team win, he certainly would have fit in well on any of Vince Lombardi's teams. I feel Lombardi would have loved him because of his tenacity and his abilities.

As a testament to his toughness, Favre has not missed a start (87 straight) since taking over for Don Majkowski in the fourth game of 1992.

THANK YOU RON WOLF
FOR BRINGING TOGETHER:

THE FATHER... THE SON... THE HOLY... & THE GHOST

Since Favre arrived in '92, Green Bay has rolled to five consecutive winning seasons and four straight playoff appearances.

More importantly, Lombardi would have loved him simply because he is a leader by example. I'm sure Lombardi would have loved to have him at quarterback.

We all know that Favre is the complete package. He not only is physical, but he has improved mentally as well, making many adjustments by reading the various defenses and picking up blitzes.

He could have fit in with the great Packer teams of the 1960s, but it's difficult to say how well he would have done. The game has changed in that it's more of a passing game now than it was in the Lombardi years. We ran the ball often behind Jim Taylor and Paul Hornung.

The rules have changed and so have the offensive blocking schemes. Today's receivers have a lot of freedom, where in the '60s they never had much freedom at all. Now you can only hold a receiver up five yards from the line of scrimmage. Defenses could be much more physical with receivers in the '60s. Even with the differences in rules, I'm sure Favre would have adjusted in the same way that Starr did.

That's pretty much how he fits into the Packer tradition. He has the confidence to do whatever it takes to win. He loves to be out there and he loves to win.

That sets him apart from a lot of other great quarterbacks. **F**

'[Brett's] a throwback type of player. Since he wants to do what he can to help his team win, he certainly would have fit in well on any of Vince Lombardi's teams.'

'I'm sure Lombardi would have loved to have [Brett] at quarterback.'

The four-time Pro Bowler and two-time MVP isn't above joking with teammates or taking a poke at head coach Mike Holmgren.

Ray Nitschke is considered by many as the greatest middle linebacker to have played in the NFL. The Hall of Famer wreaked havoc for 15 seasons (1958-72) with the Packers, helping Green Bay win five NFL championships in the 1960s and the first two Super Bowls.

The defense's inspirational leader earned many honors along the way,

including the MVP Award in Green Bay's 1962 NFL title victory over the New York Giants. In the six NFL Championship games and two Super Bowls that the Packers played between 1960 and 1968, it was the only time a defensive player was named MVP.

His teammates voted him the Most Valuable Packer in the championship year of 1967. He was named All-Pro from 1964 to '66 and earned a spot on the NFL's all-50 year and 75th anniversary teams. Nitschke was inducted into the Hall

of Fame in 1978.

The fullback and linebacker from Illinois was selected in the third round of the 1957 draft by the worst team in the NFL in the league's smallest town. He was balding, raw in skills and mean-looking, but he had an aggression that caught the eye of Vince Lombardi, who took over as head coach in 1959. Nitschke rode the bench his first three seasons before cracking the staring lineup in 1961. He quickly began to unleash his pent-up aggression and became one of the

'[Brett] could have fit in with the great Packer teams of the 1960s, but it's difficult to say how well he would have done.'

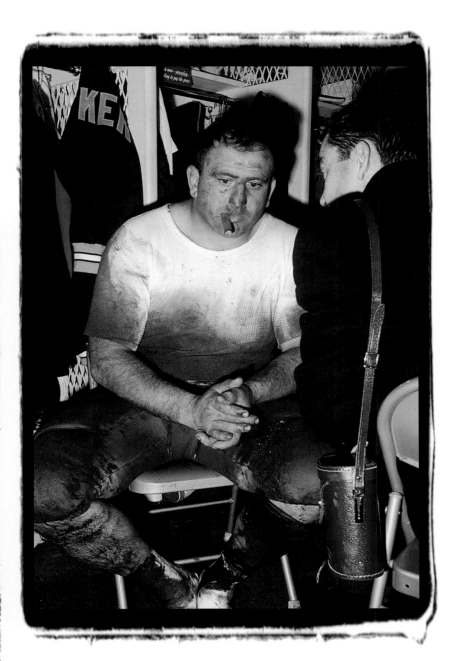

Like all great Packers players past and present, Favre not only knows how to win, but he sacrifices life and limb to do so.

more dominating middle linebackers ever. The 6-3, 235-pounder played with intensity and hit with abandon.

"I wanted to be the best football player every day, to be treated with respect," he says. "Yeah, man, I played tough."

Nitschke, 60, resides in Oneida, Wis., just west of Green Bay, and travels the country representing companies such as Champion athletic apparel, Newell and NFL Properties. He makes speaking appearances, signs autographs at card shows, plays in a number of celebrity golf tournaments and has a column in the

Packer Report, a weekly newspaper devoted to the Green Bay Packers.

In watching Brett Favre play, Nitschke is reminded of the great Packers teams of the 1960s and tough, hard-working, win-at-all-costs players such as himself, Jerry Kramer, Fuzzy Thurston, Herb Adderley, Jim Taylor and Bart Starr.

Todd Korth is the editor of Packer Report.